show
me
something
you
can
not
even
think
of

show
me
something
you
can
not
even
think
of

elena
botts

show me something you can not even think of
copyright © 2020 Elena Botts

cover art and author photo by Elena Botts

Flowstone Press,
an Imprint of Left Fork
www.leftfork.org/flowstone

First Flowstone Press Edition • March 2020
ISBN 978-1-945824-36-4

contents

i am still sitting here • 3

the inexpressible joy of being alone; virgin forest reborn • 4

I suppose you finally got away now • 5

july 30 • 7

to think the earth will outlive us • 8

i'd like to hear your voice • 9

i don't forget anything • 10

the autumn field crickets • 11

i think it must be by the tracks • 12

past the point on the water, the lighthouse is smaller • 13

winter is the remains • 14

taken out • 15

i don't like this heat and can't think much beyond it • 16

does summer end • 17

apologies for the words i kept so long • 18

build a city for me • 20

you can have me • 21

only the dead hold me • 22

i am wrong • 23

your wrist • 24

i told you • 25

the whole world is sleeping today • 26

I have mastered the art of living while asleep • 27

what anchors you to living? • 28
you come of the lay • 29
an impossible land • 30
i witness you • 32
if i missed you, would you come alive • 33
after searching for a red color in the winter woods • 34
i leave for the station • 35
in that dream, we were awake • 36
we hadn't spoken, so i wrote it down • 37
as another heartbreak passes • 38
this is how we met • 39
i am going to chicago • 41
early february • 42
the first melt of the year • 43
i want the air • 44
i feel weaker though the sickness seems to have abated • 45
northampton • 46
I don't know where to go • 47
this wound • 49
all was forgotten • 50
i often dream of peaceful resolutions • 51
the sun is setting now on my heart it seems • 52
there are many signs to m'ville but no town itself • 53
an april on the hudson • 54
the women in white • 55
our lady • 56

show
me
something
you
can
not
even
think
of

<u>i am still sitting here</u>
to watch the barges sink unholy light
will you turn the radio
we will sit in your parked car for another night

i can still sit behind the stone also
with no thought but no,
to wait for you to pronounce my name in the evening
i will listen in that shadow
to hear you asking where i have gone

where have the dreams taken these dreamers
what is it like for you downriver
i know you have such trouble with your time
and i have such trouble with mine

the sweet village sits through another burning summer
and the autumn once gave over
i will not dwell here and i will no longer i watched the stars pass over
in the muddy swamp by the bay and then came back to your room in september
i know when you think of me it will be another empty correspondence
like every word intended to dislodge

i am no longer worn to death
given like the song
as you walk in the nighttime
i was once was a ghost i know
you might see me sometimes
now i am a ghost i know
i walk from a place
but i am no longer
i am for anyone

<u>the inexpressible joy of being alone; virgin forest reborn</u>
it rains as though this were a place meant
for the wet, the river surging brown
and a white sky doesn't forget
but turns the earth a deep
and everlasting green
until we are in the thick
fabric where time passes later
yet still drags us along with it:
just another body floating down the river.

<u>I suppose you finally got away now.</u>
I don't know what to say about those stars, the bridge that doesn't exist, the house that's not haunted- and the river that you dream so much about. You can't escape to somewhere, but you could at least escape somewhere where your escapism takes on qualities of its own, where your dreams are richer and darker, where you can actually believe in your yearnings for at least a spell for at least a stretch of days when it rains and the sky is a pale grey and the greenery, a rich thick forest here, becomes enchanting or enchanted depending on the nature of your projections. This valley, it's what lies between two spirits who have passed on, it is a gift from one to the other and back again, like an unsent letter, like the pickup truck crumbling in the back of your childhood home- we're really going somewhere now, look there are boats docked here in the middle of the field- we've crossed over the ghosts that we were before. We are different ghosts now- your ancient immovable spirit is growing, or at least moving around. There's no need for quiet there's no need to talk. Everything you could've said to someone that you love- it has already been said before you've met them- you don't have to worry about it. The river is overflowing at its banks, it's a harsh brown mud water- all the animals want to drown in it. The animals will rush down to drown themselves in the river for the river is overflowing its banks on this blank day when we're all anchored in the color green. They will rush down and ride it out. There will be no blood because the blood is sucked under.

The day I cease to think of you might be a beautiful day, or it might not be, but it won't matter to me which is the problem. You must be thinking I'm faking but how could I be faking if there's nothing real, to build this lie out of. What is this thing that keeps the river running- probably something melting, up very high in those mountains- on these rainy days when the clouds come down below the highest peaks then the pieces of the sky fall down on us. It's whatever you want- I could like you a lot but I have to pretend that it's for a good reason, that I am doing my best- we're desperate for purpose which is why we stay in the house all day. I'm going to play this piano but none of the high notes work. You're going to read a book and convince me that you're doing something and that opossum outside is going to lie dead on the front doorstep and it's going to bloat and emanate an odor so intense that we have to close all the windows.

I hope you're doing well- I say that too much I hope you are walking somewhere under this grey sky as it gathers texture, moisture, in gusts deepening widening until the whole thing goes black. The stars are revealed one by one and that vacant moon which is still luminous, beautiful- buried in an undiminished sky. Love really does go on forever.

<u>july 30,</u>
if time had settled
bluer air in the summer evening
i might- call this a place again
enough to look out at the darker hill,
that is, the one beyond this one
and live like nothing, to be-
at once, inside of the room,
the creature with these illumined eyes
that wrongs all of you,
and outside, the ghost
never meant to haunt any of you.

<u>to think the earth will outlive us</u>
on the hill where the sky opened,
and we saw the infinite constellated darkness
between us, futures never lived like a dream so big
it couldn't contain itself. it was only a small dream of mine
while i am a small dream of the world.
though the structures here have been taken out,
there remain generators graffitied.
to think not long ago we stood on the porch
and watched strangers shiver.
to lie on that hill-
to see that purple distance, the horizon formed from a gradient
of forest and the mountain is made
of what is more blue.
this earth here has been too many things.
my limitation is that
i only see its immensity when i look back to see your face
looking up at the sky. though i could be that sky.
i could be the black.
a greenhouse has been newly erected
at this site out of poles and white shadows- a lattice, a tarp,
a webbed column for the mind to walk around.
inside, to grow vegetables. to cultivate nothing as could be
felt by you or me.
some other thing will be made in the ruin of a thought
or the aftermath of the greatest feeling i've known
which is so small, small
enough to contain everything.

<u>i'd like to hear your voice</u>
once you are lost, you are never found.
though it is always a summer evening,
i cannot live in it
or even think of a human, see myself in the mirror.
i know you went to sleep in the woods, the only place
you feel okay.
if you have gone away once, you have gone away forever.
when i see you at my door,
i know you are someone else again.
we spoke of many beautiful things,
you asked if i had fallen in love and i said that i hadn't
but i appreciate this time for which we've known one other
cannot last longer than the infinite hour
before you are killed
by the whole real being which knocks
as i go to the basement to conjure eternity,
to chase cats and become nothing so soon.
grandfather takes so many videos of us for this reason
now that he is gone, he walks forever.

<u>i don't forget anything</u>
you put the flowers into my pocket
i won't find them until i regret it.
you took the song out of the night sky
you didn't believe me when i said i had no thoughts
but my mind is empty
as the land, where is that land-
there is no land.
the stars could mean something
if you take them.
blessed be that which is unknown.

<u>the autumn field crickets</u>
but you are dead and no funeral
better, you are living and no life
in pursuit of so many freedoms
snuck into the carnival and swung round from a great
height
until the blur of lights neon-like
fell into the nighttime pool- finally
to float across that dark cloudy sky
without a wish

<u>i think it must be by the tracks</u>
where the river moves
immeasurably, is perfectly still
in the hollow of winter
say, in the center of the world
where the earth is white and the sky black,
the forest resonates
of the blue aura of you, shifting.
the light is left on in the chapel
where a whole
earth passes a closed breath around the sun,
this is a place without echo,
the unknown rests.

<u>past the point on the water, the lighthouse is smaller</u>
than the sails like caught birds floating when the train
rolls through the whole valley.
the ferry ferries no souls but is full of talk. we took a boat
across the surface of the sky you were so quiet like this
skeleton of glass eyes or bluer morbid pebbles. to turn and
orient towards the river
which moves more or the back creek which does less. if
only i could find you long enough to give you-
but the mountains as they are full of shroud are a
momentary heaven
and what would it be if we could grasp the sullen slopes or
heavy clouds, if we could speak about the sun
as it fell- no id rather- still dreaming you walk into my
house-
those blessings are down the road- or, i into yours- a moon
floats over water
am i so terrible i could be made only of memories, i am
afraid i could be sweet- i could walk in this field
knowing at least i will die outside when there is no one
with me
in a solitude so great the hills might reverberate into the
dark early morrows of the next-
and before, the beloved blue dusk to trace of you, which is
a universe yet to come,
and to dream a feeling is a feeling is between here and
there.
you are the only thing- as i, and the river, and the sea, sky,
and earth.

<u>winter is the remains</u>
of what was immaterial.
in this weather, the ghosts walk through-
cold water over the wrist-
two branches felled in the snow-
boxed wine they left in the back of my car-
another hook in the ceiling
or a few minutes on tarmac.
as the clouds were shot through (bursts of heaven),
a man lingers through lunch.

taken out

i dont lie here
at the mouth of the river

to walk through walls
to be immaterial

i took me out
of the world

for no good, for the sea
a world taken out of me

<u>i don't like this heat and can't think much beyond it</u>

in remembrance of the ceremonies that we held, in remembrance
of the crowds to granite
families stuck together in sweat and popsicle sticks
of the lake which is man-made to embody the
lifelessness of mid-summer late into the autumn.
so like sparse notes, people might lay out mesmerized
where there is no passage of time-
life is still water.
i am worn into the grass like its pattern on my knees
sweeter than some earlier spring blossom that might've been freed
in a wind that moves but does not speak,
as from hushed confines along the banks, a bellowing frog and the coo
or a soft mammal's howl.

<u>does summer end</u> with inches of rain,

the hospital visit as we wait
for the death of a child we never met.
i hardly know how to suffer through this type of caring
i am so quiet now, so beyond imagining.
i collected some flowers on the way to your house
and dropped them along the road
so you wouldn't find me too much.

after the show, you stood outside in the rain, reading.
they all smoke the same cigarettes here.
i am afraid i cannot tell you another story after this one.
the holy people have ordained themselves, i am afraid
there are no white horses to cross the water
and in the end, no animals like to be ridden
and slaughtered.

i gave you a few days to put your thoughts together,
to take the feelings from where they have arisen
and pour out into the garden like some everlasting rain
that soon dissipates as the kettle whistles
of a certain kind of air that escapes,
its admittances placed in cups like small catastrophes.

would you walk out of paralysis, one leg over the bed,
meaning to move but unsure of space and time still
but for this and that monitor. at least they removed the sheet
that covered your body so you can, once more, feel the temperature.

<u>apologies for the words i kept so long</u>, and then
showed you like a child humming along, over the
balcony over the man eating his lunch. circled, you are
afraid of bees- are you really afraid of so many things
and do not look me in the eye? i cannot believe-

when you shook for that someone on the phone, the
someone we do not know and yet, you were there for.
should i have invented some new and gentle motion
in mimicry of a phasing moon, here is my wound, a
hole in the sky in fatal appreciation, a conflagration,
shall we say, in honor of your terrible kindness? oh
look, another shift in the heavens which then wax and
settle as if i could tell the story i know, from end to
beginning too-

your face is always changing shape but the shapes
within it never reconcile the pale green eyes are beyond
imagining, a crooked nose, pierced, narrow cheeks
and chin and mouth, slender and awkward in bearing
a creature of always escaping from the pool, jumping
the fence at midnight or huddled is this a different
sort of shivering, trees in nonexistent wind i find
unnecessarily but still i find you and in looking- is
there that quiet space that i have discovered, you keep
it so well. i wish i could, make an evening move from
sundown to blackness by watching you, your corners
and in corners, to pay attention, to find that which
renders you transfixing, to soothe in deadly calm the
straight muscles of your back and never to stop gazing
at the face which never stops gazing outward and to
decipher the sweet nonsense from your shoulders

onward and again to render motionless the strange knees, the conflictory essence of you, the tied roots and striations of veins most visible in your hands and feet, all this knowing the body is nothing, all this a pretense for meaning, a vessel made to send a message, here, friend, is the message- one of unutterable care, i am devastated by you

<u>build a city for me</u>, where the lone man can walk, still alone
without even the little trails to the river
only the open carriage of a freight bearing
the sound of a whistle, weightless
sorrow is as crafts
carried over water, a ring of oars
and i forget the rest. grant me a solitude so immense
i cannot even know what it is to think-
i am already there, it is as useless as that isle
beloved between the banks
of a deadly flourishing tide
in the aftermath of sweet trespasses
soon will not be remembered, only kept in the soil
only a soul's stones and ruin
or the sky held in the quarry pool. i had visions of you
like this here and there rain,
no, i had nothing
but an view through the center of the world. here is the place
i died,
here is my haunting-grounds.
you are free to walk here, it could be
anywhere on earth for the end is no deeper
than the beginning, they are the same
lamplights glowing like stars unconstellated,
cast along the mouth of the bay.

<u>you can have me</u>, use me for this thick purpose
open and close as crickets do, reading the fine veins of weather
as pulse and tell a slow articulation of the fall.
i can walk through walls, read minds.
these interiors are as quiet as the river as heard from the high
building or the bridge or the sky
or in the wide deadening night.
i am always wrong
as bodies are made to be, so carefully bloody.
so take me out, as a ghost from the window joins the wind.
shake the curtains,
i wanted you to kill me
but this is a poor autopsy.
i've got to honor a few things on the 13th of september:
even the oblivion he offered me
is too soon forgotten i think, no night will ever be so dark
as through the window of the little neon restaurant on one corner of the crossroad,
as after the day you took off for the city wanting no small tokens- you were still unrealized, you are still unable
as in the breath of a moment passing from one to
the other- the moon, a poet, no one- sorry for all the information.
here is something that lasts forever.
you'll never remember quite what it was like.
remind me of something for a time now it is over.
so here is the pale era, when needlessly, we row backwards the waters of the mind-
you might feel okay
or that great echoing sound:
such blue worlds.

<u>only the dead hold me</u>

me, a child with mouth and eyes open, he looking up with wonderment, a grandfather...
or me, in that meadow outside the stadium, in the grass you search with your hands to bind me up in something but i escape..
or you, too soon i know but now that the living room is painted yellow and i must place you on your bed, you with that great power as it ebbs into the next....
and lest i forget the animals...
and the man that once taught me many fine and minute things who took pictures of my grandmother and the rolls she would bake as i listened for the other worlds signified by the sound of chimes beyond the window...

oh thank god for this wild earth that speaks no language, for the trees that move in every breeze and the river which goes and goes and there is nothing greater than that i cannot fathom the sea

<u>i am wrong</u>, i think, as i was then when he snuck into my room through the window which had been open to that great night air in that cool autumn of my dreams but did he really sneak in? the most beautiful things i have seen are gone and it would not do to take them. here is something that lasts forever. you'll never remember quite what it was like. nightly, his sweet corpse- still unrealized, still unable. and again, when i was taken into surrender as though to end those last few bearings upon this earth and my apologies especially for being a ghost around her too, you are far better than i am. i wish mostly i could show you the value i see in you but you mind that so it is sorrow worse to have taken these words and spaces, to pretend meanings and to walk through minds, perhaps my own. i might be wrong in marrow as i am the one without hope, that is true as without hope there is no struggle and i have no struggle and you have that great thing, life. i knew because i cried for a quiet spell and like those winking lights of the barges as they drift by silently i am moved but cannot move and so think, oh thank god for this wild earth that speaks no language, thank god that we can hardly fathom the sea, though probably i can fathom anything that would take me into something real, or better, take me apart until i knew what it was to not be. i might be taking that train knowing finally how to step out of time, knowing my dearest friend and i had finally said goodbye. to make the word gone a new word, to say, i am.

<u>your wrist</u> thrown out of the worn garment,
for this smoke in the morning,
you drink hot water after,
in the autumn cool
one remembers what one is, a specter
of love, i am cold all the time.

<u>i told you</u> it was a reminder of all existence, this- the slightest ribcage as if untouched by the world or the breath of a bird, or to caress that fleeting vision of me, you were sure to "let me know": a dark and distant sea, my unknown weather. i come sometimes back to the haunted livingston to linger deep in a thought of your careful trespasses, your unconscionable veneration.

<u>the whole world is sleeping today</u>, the horizon is not pronounced, i want to dwell in that erasure. i am estranged from feeling, though there is always some memory to cry over. the spirit comes back.

<u>I have mastered the art of living while asleep.</u> It is possible, however, that I will forget what it is to be awake. So once a week, I wake for a day or so where the sky is clear and the land runs wild as my mind. In six weeks, I will consider a new means of passing time. I may be later than the hour of the end; I wish I were far past no night or morning.

<u>what anchors you to living?</u>
sorrow, devotion to an outside,
love gone now, but
the hills, the hills that frostbitten contemplation of self destruction
better, that thing beyond thinking
o, well, stillness now! silence now! sleep!,
should i make a silent album:
i'm here
i'm listening
i'm open to anything you have to say
no, too trite, too nothing,
exactly what i have criticized about art before- an idea without true development, realization
this place, you know it is a deep blessing.

<u>come of the lay</u>
you come, rain-soaked, of the lay
of an impossible land.
composed of open spaces,
i am made of vast distances.
you have become human, lately.
i have become less of anything.
would you worry me a place,
even being is disgrace.
i'd seek every kind of freedom,
joyous, go forth to my ruin,
dwelling in bones set by sorrows
eternal, every star sets it is forever.
the deepest light i'd ever seen
extinguished though it was no dream.

<u>an impossible land</u>
if we could pull that moon down i think we might be better off
i might walk out this morning
and never come back again
in all these faces i am still looking for you
when i see you i don't recognize
that space where we saw the end
near the indian burial ground
i had to call you and you came to get me
we did not have many birthdays spent together how unfortunate
we could pull those stars down
i know how you take all from i would not have you rearrange our distances
i liked those distances
i'd rather not talk about the hills
where i could wander forever
until i reached a clear lake with all the sky within its surface
there are a few things i'd rather not talk about
i'd rather keep to myself
like the day it snowed on my birthday waiting for a train that didn't come
some of us are just more comfortable with nothing
some would rather not be part of this strange system of living
i hear there's a promised land i hear no one lives there and it's always winter
you could take my body out if i don't reach there
you could take my body out if i reach there
take me out

by the time the ice forms we will be going to the bigger
continent in search of displacements
in search of desolation there is no consolation
i remember thinking you were the stuff of angel's dreams
i wanted to rescue your body from the snow
the sun now is setting on my heart it seems

<u>i witness you</u>, as i have never seen before, your happy destructions
different, shuttered light vacancies of mind
you have spectacular incendiary ways
especially in the morning
could carry a dream far aloft
you looked small. i ravaged, myself, as the hills ought to have done
as that setting autumnal sun.
i think i might give myself up without a sound
i lie, for many nights and days, you take one step into the world and another out
acute sorrows that come
with regaining certain feelings towards things in the outside world. i am spent,
full of devotions that fall out of the frame.
not fit even for denial,
i succumb to doubt.
i recognized surrender and held that sorrow, my skeleton was made of it
when i saw you, i fell out thinking
maybe you're figuring out how to live and care about it.
you have no sacrifice or the possibility of something worthwhile
i do not mind though i am cold as the weather turns
this is the sort of love that kills me.
i could show you
uncompromising adoration, a sacrifice that gives way
if only i were to undo your suffering, send you away.

<u>if i missed you, would you come alive</u>
do you feel snow before it falls in the night sky
the dead dream of a better place
to live separate unapologetic lives
if we find it, then can we die
you might be divine, ah, you might be divine
i said i wanted to be here long enough
to give myself up in love and sorrow
to all the people that passed by
and then without a wish,
i could leave, guiltless
to pass my own eternal moment.

<u>after searching for a red color in the winter woods,</u>
i encountered the twigged stillness of those naked trees
and the living static, silence of ice
like a new form of breathing-
i might be content also to lie half asleep in sorrow and
pull away thinking my ghosts look so good today-
dim as the sun, a hole in the grey-
here is the door at the end of the world; it stays open.

<u>i leave for the station.</u> it must be winter. the capitol is silent. today, it is a good day to "walk around". i realize many deep sorrows, again. i gaze out across an empty nation. i am happy to be blind. dear universe when i have given all my love, obliterate me. i cut my hair and achieved boyhood. i have no poetry but this… people turn to stare at the pigeons flapping through mcdonalds. it is hard to say, because the ocean is so big.

<u>in that dream, we were awake,</u>
there was no clothing the feeling.
i went out and down the street
in the lavender daylight of early winter,
walking past the steps of houses
and through electrical wires
all the way down to the bay
where the last warmth of sunlight was revealing
some other sphere of being.
i returned to your home but i realized
you too were outside of believing
i had always walked the earth alone
and could only hear my breathing.
i woke and you were gone,
but in my house women were cleaning.
in the pale depths of early morning,
like a chorus of ghosts,
i walked outside.

we hadn't spoken, so i wrote it down

i treasure you, i- adore your soul, i love the way you care for the world. i love your braveries and your fragilities, these which are so linked. i like to listen to your thoughts, i like your awarenesses, your insights, your obfuscations. i am guilty to admit how often i have in dreams consciously and unconsciously considered you, touched your mind, thought of the depths and latitudes of your existence, both in the finite bends which are like some small incidental testament to your hours, your living, the strange narratives of bones and veins and skin, and a face which is to me, intimate, kind, something a soul moves in and out of, and also your otherwordly motion, but mostly that which is illimitably you, your soul, which seems a distant and benevolent light, i cannot say if i felt more like you were some holy child i wish i could care for or if seeing you is like a romance that i endure the ambiguity of, afraid that were i to tell you, you also might suffer from something that rends and rends and takes no sure path but this, and i am thankful also for your friendship because it grants me the place to sit with you through the slow passage of time and i like to be here for you, very, very much. this is undoubtedly a love poem from someone who cannot know anything of love except in particular degrees i have tried to articulate, perhaps i am both intense and limited, perhaps i bring only doubt and sorrow, but i wish i could take you to the place at the end of the world where everything has already happened, "far past no night or morning", i wish i could give you my love like it was some deepest blessing, and then i might go away with that separate and complete peace of one soul honoring another.

<u>as another heartbreak passes</u>, i wish i cared for someone and that it was worthwhile and good for them and that love was not a reoccuring tormenting dream or a useless heartfelt thought or a dark nighttime walk in the cold from nowhere to nowhere, or worse, an unconscionable burden for someone else because i like best to sit in this place alone and could pass a lifetime in admiration of the beauty of the hills especially, or of anything, but then i become afraid i have no purpose in being fixed with a form in this world (but of course all sweet sentiments become sufferings, losses are inevitable but do not erase that great original feeling which is again so particular each time)

<u>this is how we met</u>
we met at a party and you came up to me and burned
my hand with a cigarette and i shied away but later
we were in a group of people who went to a clear black
lake and we got separated from the rest and i had to
show you the way back and you said this was nice
and gave me your number but when i texted it no one
answered. but actually we met on the internet and you
called me so i came to new jersey to sit with you in a
bus station.
or, we met in a diner and i knew you as soon as i saw
you which was awkward because i had to introduce
myself again and i followed you onto the subway and
we sat together in silence before you brought me back
to your apartment we both thought about getting off
the train at any stop and never seeing each other again
but you said you wanted to talk to me as you feel
asleep.
we met on the train tracks after i gave you a few cents
so you came to my haunted old house to peer out the
window curiously all through the night and we woke
to go to the general store and sit outside, you with
your coffee, me with my nothing but a look and feeling
of morning.
we met on the porch as you smoked in front of me and
later i admired your contour at the bus stop and as you
lay in the grass in the predawn.
we met in the basement of a house as you ate i
described to you the birds i had seen that reminded me
of you though i did not know you yet and later you
kissed my hand and ran away somewhere outside of
this waking universe.

we met because you smiled like a madman, and your silhouette reminded me of someone else until we sat facing each other under the auspices of the chocolate factory one summer night which gave way to many years.
we met because i shared some story of heartbreak and you shared yours and you said that there were many more people to meet, as we sat on the steps in that night before i went away.
we met on the first day of the new year as the palest morning came into being.
in the beginning i was not there, so where were they with love, without love? they were all forgotten stars, and it was okay. the universe had got them. in the beginning, they already knew the ending but still they were afraid. even in the beginning, i loved you and i told you this but you were not there and i had never met you and maybe hardly knew you so my words were for no one and didn't matter but regardless, i said it.
now i'm in my bed feeling ribs snow outside making light white inside as though everything has already been seen and felt the meaning of the word exhausted.

<u>i am going to chicago</u>, i am more tired than ever in the halls that are smaller and smaller beneath the capitol, i think kindly of you, i feel something about you, i am falling out of the world- and so soon- but have things to do, a house to make or find in the country to be alone corporeally as well as in my mind, i send out devotions in unmarked envelopes, praying for a gentle ending to come soon

<u>early february</u>
i cannot live through the middle of the day,
i am waiting around to die, i must go out and out
show me something i cannot even think of

you showed me something i cannot even think of,
three deer through the light shadow of the wood
just now the lake is zero degrees

you are involuntary, sleep is measured in shivers
through a pale hour, this pale hour?
a house, a road, a place in the forest-
all this in the snow, which holds depth
and gives nothing

i'd like to meet you sometime, i say,
the part of you that isn't spoken
by the blue mind of your heart

you meet me somewhere, here
as you take the hour apart
you are like a being is,
the spine of the world,
the death that we are all coming to
it is sad to know
that you are so beautiful

when did you come apart from the world
you are one breath past this impossible plain
as the sun dips and rises,
as the birds fall into a row and scatter

<u>the first melt of the year,</u>
a hunger to turn the earth over
you are a prince on the fire escape,
looking out to find that the branches, the roof,
the cold gutted and dripping
just shoulders and back as you ask me to come with you
no, i stay in your room alone for two nights
hiding in the shadows through the day,
going out into the snow at night
you left the heater on while you were away
as the room turns into the glow
i wish i could but i do not wish
to feel a way about your besotted form
i am followed now, not by foxes,
but by this present effigy of the self
as it forms out of the now,
without reference to
an old photograph
of me awaiting some distant train
i want to return only to that platform
i burn like a wax figurine, blessed with too much
and for no god either
as though i might find a space in the world
but i was never made

<u>i want the air</u>, the first light and the last, the brief eclipsing forms as fall out over the river, whatever comes off the river, in the night, that night when you fell into nothing-- the unimaginable! o, some living death in the vault of open air, some suffering as from the silences through which still the river moves, losing to the shoreline in waves, love is forgetting you, the thought in which we are all submerged, the mind of the world is open.

<u>i feel weaker though the sickness seems to have abated</u>
i raise the window shade thinking about a gentle
obliteration
each day a half life to be survived and tucked away
beneath the sheet like the asphyxiation of a care,
my circulation is poor enough that my feet are cold in
the warm house, under the blanket
i will put the rest of my memories in the box on the
dresser in the room
to take out and hold as the night ends
my dreams becoming
more and more vivid
let me hide in this house a moment longer
to write out these apologies
over and over, until my hands bleed
which is like a feeling, to be made of blood is not
repentance
i will never
grow accustomed to the small hurts i may or may not
have sown
in you or you i'm afraid
if i've wasted your holiness, a kiss to the brow,
i have no place in this world

<u>northampton</u>
i am thinking that i died recently and in the morning
the snow was melting outside the window into a fog as
rises from the world,
which will remain asleep for a few days after
where you live in a little white room with a few
belongings and your wrist splayed over the side
of the bed as you dream but this i did not see because i
was in a different dream somewhere beside your dream
and i wondered whether you were unconditional like a
fragment of the world taken out
too fragile, i could not-
id like to know you-
as though you were made
only of love and surrender.

<u>I don't know where to go</u>. I am like a being is- I don't know where to go. I don't know. I don't think I should be. I don't think. You ruined me- no, I did. There are no happy love affairs. It is sad to know that you are so beautiful. I feel as though I broke something beautiful. All I give, is grief. He is, afraid of his sins- he killed a man and god will forgive him. I watch as the horse is slaughtered. I watch as the horse wanders. I see the blood, from the neck. Such a deep red surging outward, everywhere. The blood pours as the skin of the neck falls empty. He says god will forgive him and smiles up at the madonna. Can she really bear all of our sins, he wonders- elysium is not like how you think. You must not forgive yourself, only god will- the head of the horse is skinned, the head of the horse is white. I drove my car to go and see you- I dreamt of a spring that would open like the wind does, carry me out over the river- I had many plans, like the spring light that erupts just green and distant, the sky's pale introspection, a thought of summer, or something greater, of a time that does not kill for nothing- I killed a man. Should I silence myself, though it smells of wax, the candle lit by my mother and her lover in the next room- blood all over my back, blood as the day I was born- I don't so much want to speak any longer. You can sit in my room but I don't so much want to speak any longer. I don't want to hurt you, or anyone. I was not meant. I have no room, no space in the world but your grief I might hold- whose grief I might hold? Anyone's. I am open. I would hold the ache for you if it would make you feel that you could love, beyond yourself. There is a place where everything has gone. It is called a ruin.

I might live there, and here also, in the room they have left behind, which is so miraculously empty. And we lay with the dead, thinking. As I lay with the dead, living, I am grateful to you, for you are somewhere out there, existing. I hope someday I too will be forgotten, and I wish my love for you would not be so lost, but there is no redemption, only loss. Over the phone, tell me one last story about your day.

o, <u>this wound</u>, this bright unbearable wound
the wound of the heart, i knew from the wind which
took us,
not lightly out past the shoreline-
as another day passes on the endless shore-
but farther, deeper into affliction,
the opaque tide which comforts like some easy death.

is it that dear river, the one that my thoughts flow
through
that my dreams rise from as mist along the lowland
and any feeling as could melt from the hills
on this one long equinox as the weather turns
and the earth comes open
raw and muddied and stricken with life.

it is beyond any blessing,
to be unloved, to rise dripping.
in the end, of course
it will all be over.

<u>all was forgotten</u>; as acquaintances in a coffee shop in fact; a dream that we met again; no ill will; no pull; stranger to myself and yourself, who comes and then goes; to put to rest (the poem about there being no grave); kids collapsing false intimacies like milk cartons in the backyard; the great river severed in struts of the rip van winkle; lovelessly; not to watch me wash blood from my hands as i had watched him in the bathroom of keene; before the unconscionable killing of the two deer i saw through your bedroom window; an idealized peaceful resolution; not some cry to the madonna; bare of any feeling as could be imagined; or we met for the first time; a series of dreams repeating: we never met

<u>i often dream of peaceful resolutions</u>; the way rivers come apart; no ill will; no pull; walking home after some long ago conversation or moonless night; mutual understanding; a memory of sitting in the field in the duskening autumn; an acknowledgement of the parting of friends; no great feeling except for the land or a forgiveness i have not earned; my gratitude if it did not burn

<u>the sun is setting now on my heart it seems</u>
tall grass all turned to gold, a mountainside
the facade of main street shops empty of the city people,
hudson resumes its last incarnation: ghost town,
past industries a creak in the wind, or other sounds found
out by the wind
the spark and hiss of the stopped freight, its light a low
yellow, the load stopped for miles
the swinging gate,
as the train passes, the death i could've had goes after
the basketballs echoing from the youth penitentiary
rottweiler racing around the yard in pursuit of what
that church of redemption silent, only one window lit
we might live in two shacks out on the water
but the ghosts who live in them have not yet finished
their time
before the soft obliterating waves
from a ferry that passes on upriver
i linger again under the rip van winkle
thinking of how the struts open to a new kind of sky
when we meet will we dismantle
the fading light illusory,
these woods only deepen in the night
do you not think the beautiful thing will hurt you
of course the beautiful thing will hurt you
until you wake sometime after the end
to do it all again

<u>there are many signs to m'ville but no town itself</u>
it is
one hill after another

lately, i'm unable
though the outer world is so captivating
in this morning i could sit in the sun
this april has no secrets budding,
only the mud of yesterday it snowed

a host of my own thoughts which
are deeper worlds than any
i am enamored, anyway with the hills
i am just, resting

on the road i had the strange thought i may not love
anything
life is to invent a want and hold
death as i was coming away and then back towards
and still to go on differently

on the back of the sunday freight
to return to that stone i sat on, telling you this is
where i began
like sin, moths that swarm
along the banks
now that it is warm,
we can grow nothing and let the world do the rest,
turn green and etcetera

i know in living i grow fainter
like a body
resting on the unsentimental river
carried down, that is something

<u>an april on the hudson</u>
i thought you had
come and gone
as ghosts are wont to do
i already waved at the ferrygoers from the bank of the river

i am ill, as ever, mostly bedridden but hope to see the sky soon
i woke once in the small hours as if to find some devil
instead there was a slow-moving freight
moving down the avenue
shaking the houses awake

now that i am here among the living,
the wind reaches no destination,
that is what wind is
only the light is different now, the sky opens
as the sun falls
i think of death incessantly
it makes tasks more difficult
they drank from these cups and left them behind
i do not know where this blood comes from,
so i clean the kitchen
it is sad that we must all contain many cruelties

unrequited is a great blessing
the flower that never blossoms never closes
illusions may remain intact
and every small service may be rendered as though for something greater
i have always been monastic
but what is devotion without a higher power
a small number of steps towards the shore
and away again

<u>the women in white</u>
to be a woman is nothing
it is young lady and then it is màm
to be a man, that is something, it is sir
and the coat we have forgotten
in the house of the friend we do not speak to any
longer.
to be the child is to be the holy spirit,
and then go missing.
i only like female men, for they have confused too
many things.
you can wear white when you ask to be forgiven
and the sky will forgive you, and the wood,
and the moon will forgive you,
until you are alone and unjustified
in yourself and such doubt forms at the core
of your being and you are cast back
into the unimaginable, as you always were,
unremitting.

i thought, we will come to an end on the shore
i thought i would surprise myself
when we came to the end on the shore
and we came to the shore
in the fog, in the dark
on the banks of the river
and i was only surprised in the way i am surprised
when i know what it is that is coming
what was the light from behind that fog?
where did it come from, in the dark?

<u>our lady</u>

the church is burning
and the funeral parlor the boy I once knew lived in,
long after the sad aftermaths
the yearnings from berlin
or even past the lifetimes of those white swans circling
the island in the wien.
soon it will all be put to rest,
I will not be resurrected (I hope)
by some madman as the other elena was,
though we all shall carry on as some glass corpse
falsely held and seen.

it is ok here, now
I know that the creaking sound is from the sign
hanging
above the storefront
and that I live in apartment number three
and sometimes, as I walk past my room,
I recognize that someone must be living there
the bed is unmade, a lamp illuminates
a white sheet space.

outside the house one can hear the conversation from
inside
and also the birds and the chime
marked by the wind and the sun it scatters
any feeling as could be had.
it is an indifferent universe, a press to the doorbell,
a waiting for that unopened.

or as my mom says,
"second half day better-
I went to a beach restaurant with T-
physical therapy very painful and I don't like pain
meds."

I dangle the phone above the couch
that I sit on with the perfect angle of the same bird
being part of the sun,
which is new, as it is easter
now in the valley.

about the author

Elena Botts has lived in the Hudson Valley, Johannesburg, Berlin, NYC, DC, and many other places. In the past few years, her poems have been published in dozens of literary magazines. She is the winner of four poetry contests and has had six books published. Her visual artwork has won numerous awards and has been exhibited in various galleries. She has also collaborated on, released and exhibited sound and moving image art.

www.ingramcontent.com/pod-product-compliance
Lightning Source LLC
Chambersburg PA
CBHW050334120526
44592CB00014B/2176